Answered Prayer

Answered Prayer

By Lola Allen

ARPress

ILLUMINATING IDEAS
EMPOWERING VOICES

ARPress
45 Dan Road Suite 5
Canton MA 02021

Hotline: 1(888) 821-0229
Fax: 1(508) 545-7580

Ordering Information:
Quantity sales. Special discounts are available on quantity purchases by corporations, associations, and others. For details, contact the publisher at the address above.

Printed in the United States of America.

ISBN-13: Softcover   979-8-89676-248-5
          Hardcover   979-8-89676-250-8
          eBook   979-8-89676-249-2

Library of Congress Control Number: 2025903076

Table of Contents

Book Dedication

I dedicate this book to God.

For He has spared my life on many occasions. Thus, I am here today to tell the world of my story and my personal encounter with Him.

To my granddaughter Racquel Brown.

I thank you for spending endless time taking me to and from my doctors' appointments when I physically could not drive myself. Thank you for shopping for me and thank you for spending your days off with me. Working full-time and sacrificing the time it took to create the multiple drafts of the book, I know was not easy. Thank you. Any success of this book is due partly to you. I love you dearly. May God continue to bless and keep you.

To my son, James Brown, and ex-wife, Joy.

To Sister Roslin Pickney.

Thank you for making sure I had food to eat; like a mother tending to her child. I pray that God also continues to bless you and your family always. May your storehouse never run dry.

To the men that helped saved my life.

Thank you for diverting traffic away from my car. Thanks for pulling me out and preserving my life as best you could until the ambulance could rescue me. I never did catch either of your names, nor have I been able to thank you personally. It is never too late! If you read this book, please contact me. I would like to thank you personally. God bless you both. I truly believe you were sent by God as my angels of protection. Thank you!

Hubert Alphonso Allen

Racquel Brown

Acknowledgments

I would like to thank the doctor that attended to me first, upon entry into the trauma unit at Jackson Memorial Hospital. Thank you for your professionalism and patience in explaining procedures to me. Before you intervened, I was refusing treatment that ultimately made saving my life easier and possible.

My sincerest gratitude to the entire unit that was responsible for the reconstruction of my ribs. For the time spent locating the five ribs that were broken, drilling holes, cutting titanium strips and shaping them to my ribcage, I thank you all. May God be with you all. May He bless you in addition to your families. And if I never get to thank you personally, may I be able to in heaven.

Thanks to all the nurses and unit secretaries in the hospital that took care of me. I am unable to recall you all by name, but God bless you. To the respiratory unit that treated me around the clock to ensure that I could breathe while my lungs were collapsed, I will always remember your faces. Specifically, the face of the respiratory therapist smiling at me and saying, "Sister Allen you're going to be okay."

Mr. Lloyd Oats, you will never know how appreciated your work is. Thank you and God bless you.

Sister Gibson, thank you for your early contributions in the creation of this book.

Thank you to all the staff at the Jewish Home Hospital where I completed rehab. Thanks for helping me to be able to walk and return home again.

Thank you to my church sisters Elene John Lewis and Escantie for your roles in my recovery.

To the members of North Side Seventh-Day Adventist Church. Thank you for the daily visits and for praying with and for me. Your encouragement assisted me in many ways that you'll never understand. Thank you, Pastor T. McNealy, Sister Daphnis, and Roslin Pickney. And thank you to anyone else whose name escapes me during this process.

To my sister Carol and her church family, thank you for taking the time to come and visit with me.

It is virtually impossible for me to remember all the names that played a role in my recovery, but you all know who you are. God will bless you for all that you have done for me.

To my family and friends, thank you. Also, to my neighbor who never forgot to visit me with a helping hand.

Introduction

This happened years before my accident. I used to work as a private duty nurse and I would frequently get paid by the patient or the patient's family. One day I was going to pick up a check from a home in Coral Cables. As I left my home, the radio in the car started playing a song, "For you I am praying. I am praying for you."

I burst into tears and began to sob loudly. I had to pray. It had suddenly dawned on me that my earthly father had just died and I was now alone. I had no one praying for me anymore. I felt so lonely and I cried bitterly all the way from NW 95th street to SW 110th street. Before I knew it, I had forgotten where I was going. So, I turned my car into a driveway and stopped there. I looked around trying to identify where I was. The place was bright. It was like looking in a View-Master. The trees were sugarcane and the bananas looked so pretty, like a brightly colored picture. Once I got myself together and looked at the address, it turned out I was exactly where I needed to be. I had to take a moment to stop and pray yet again. Jesus brought me all the way to my destination. I cried more and harder. I opened my eyes and the place looked normal. It wasn't such a pretty picture anymore. I went into the house. The people inside were very friendly and had my check waiting for me. I received it. And I thanked them and went home. On the entire drive back, all I could do was thank God for his love and mercy. He carried me safely to my destination. I do not know how or why, but God is always with me.

He is there during the moments of joy and sorrow. He is there when I'm in pain and sickness. He never leaves me. My mother and father are now deceased. I have only God. He is always with me even when I was a child. He was always there to talk to when I was sad, alone, or unhappy. He never left me throughout my entire life. And when I was in school struggling to make the grades, He was there. But Jesus

115   I Am Praying for You.

S. O'Maley Cluff.

Ira D. Sankey.

M. 100

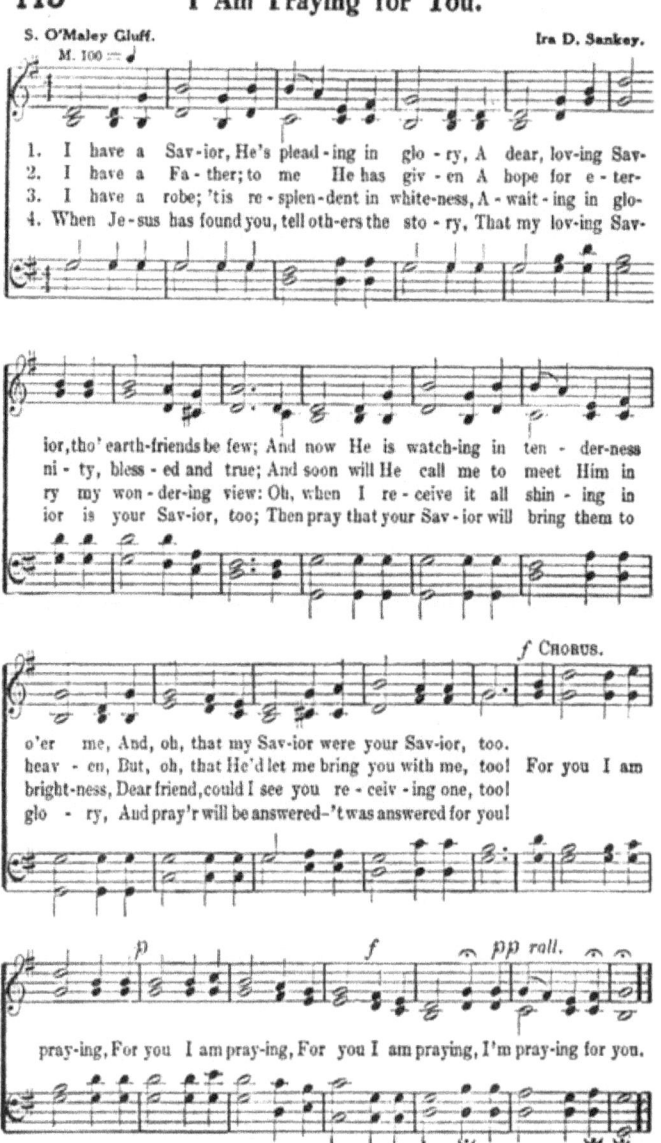

1. I have a Sav-ior, He's plead-ing in glo - ry, A dear, lov-ing Sav-
2. I have a Fa - ther; to me He has giv - en A hope for e - ter-
3. I have a robe; 'tis re - splen-dent in white-ness, A - wait - ing in glo -
4. When Je-sus has found you, tell oth-ers the sto - ry, That my lov-ing Sav-

ior, tho' earth-friends be few; And now He is watch-ing in ten - der-ness
ni - ty, bless - ed and true; And soon will He call me to meet Him in
ry my won - der-ing view: Oh, when I re - ceive it all shin - ing in
ior is your Sav-ior, too; Then pray that your Sav - ior will bring them to

f Chorus.

o'er me, And, oh, that my Sav-ior were your Sav-ior, too.
heav - en, But, oh, that He'd let me bring you with me, too! For you I am
bright-ness, Dear friend, could I see you re - ceiv - ing one, too!
glo - ry, And pray'r will be answered-'t was answered for you!

p   f   pp rall.

pray-ing, For you I am pray-ing, For you I am praying, I'm pray-ing for you.

keep me even when I became a mother and had no one to turn to. He had my back during the difficult times of childbearing when I was alone and had no help. Now that I can reflect and look back at how I made it, I ask myself how I could have done it without God. I raised three boys without their father and only those who have gone through it could understand what that was like. God gave me the strength to make a choice and bear my cross alone. And with His grace, I survived the ups and the downs. Now, I am a grandmother and a great-grandmother. I am still living day by day with the help of Jesus, the Holy Spirit, and my God.

The day God came down and covered me and kept me alive, He touched me and spoke to me. I will always remember that day, Thursday, October 1, 2009 at approximately 2:00 p.m.

By now, we've all heard people telling their life's stories and about their personal encounters with God. Usually, they recount dying and then going to heaven. They claim to have seen God. Well, I believe it's true because it happened to me. Not the same way, but I saw God! I didn't die. I never witnessed this tunnel of bright, white light. I wasn't miraculously transported to heaven. It all took place right here on earth that I saw God in person. He touched me on my forehead with His hand. I could feel four of His fingers. He spoke in my ear. I heard His soft voice and gently He asked me a question. I had to stop and ask myself, *was that God I just saw?* In my moment of questioning, He answered me verbally just as I speak to my closest acquaintances. His voice was tender and shocked me. I could never forget it as long as I live. I can't wait to get to heaven because once I'm there I plan to hug him and thank him for saving my life when I was dying on Interstate 95 back in 2009.

Think about how you would have responded to the presence of the Almighty. Would you jump up and shout? Would you scream for joy? Put yourself in my position for a minute. You are in the presence of the

Lola Allen

Creator of this world; divine, holy, and sinless God. And me, just a sinner that deserves to die in His presence. Somehow, I am still alive to tell about it. Whenever I think about that day, I get chills knowing that I am still here. Why did He choose to descend and save me from dying?

8

The Morning Before the Day I should Have Died

It was October 1. I was going to work the 3:00-11:00 p.m. shift at Jackson Memorial Hospital. I had worked there for twenty-eight years. This was a day like none other. The sun was shining brightly. The sky was blue and there was not a cloud in the sky. I can remember the morning temperature being quite cool. I had an appointment with ADT Home Security to fix my alarm. The young man who came to do the work had a peculiar appearance. I showed him the room where my unit was. He came back out and told me I had to pay him taxes on the price the company offered me to do the work and that if I did not, he was not going to do the work. I became upset and called the company. We had a discussion and the atmosphere changed in the house. Something was wrong!

A record was playing Christian songs, the same songs I listened to every day. I could hear the words of the songs. I kept telling myself not to let this incident cause me to lose my joy. I could sense that evil had entered my space. I asked him to leave and he did. But when he went in the room and came out, I am not sure what took place. His appearance was strange, and I felt different when he spoke to me. I felt angry for no good reason. I didn't know that day I would not return home for five weeks and it was a miracle that God saved my life. When I think back on what happened that day, my spirit bid me send the young man away and out of my home. But the damage was done. Evil was at work to hurt me. But God intervened and sent two angels to protect me. Later on that same day, He would have to save my life.

I got dressed for work and had some errands to run. It was about noon. I went to the Village El Portal to pay for my permit for my alarm. After that I went to Walgreens drugstore to pick up my blood pressure medications. As I left the store, I got on the expressway to head to work at Jackson Memorial Hospital. Just as I was entering the highway, I heard a loud sound coming from behind me. It got louder and louder as it was coming up behind me. At first, it sounded like several bikes; motorcyclists.

I glanced back to see what it was and noticed it was a truck. I was trying to get away from the sound when suddenly I felt a hard thump at my back-left door. Everything changed from that moment on. I prayed, "Lord, I am hit. Please do not let me die up here!" The moment I called on Jesus to take control, He had already planned to save my life. He knew that the Evil One had planned to take my life and had provisions for me—not one, but two angels—to protect me from oncoming cars. Imagine a car careening across three lanes without colliding with any others on a busy causeway. My thoughts wandered. "Why weren't there any cars coming?" The traffic was moving as usual with all four lanes filled. Vehicles were everywhere before I started praying to God about not allowing other cars to hit me. The moment I felt the thump I said, "Lord please do no let me die up here." I kept praying, "Lord please take control." The car wanted to spin in circles. I had to struggle to keep it steady on the road. I kept asking God, "Why I am not seeing any cars coming?" When I saw that I was about to hit the wall, I turned my head to the side and closed my eyes. *Job 33:17-28* My car went out of control. The more I tried to go straight, the car insisted on turning left and wanting to turn around and over. I struggled with the steering, but the car continued to head across three lanes and into the median.

Not a cloud was in the sky. All day the sun had been shining brightly. Driving safely as I usually do, I entered the I-95 expressway at Northwest 95th Street. Suddenly I heard a loud sound coming from behind me. I glanced back to see what it was. There I noticed that it was a truck; a Mack truck. The next thing I felt was a bump to my back-left door. Then I said, "Oh, my Lord I am hit!"

My car swirled and started going across the lane. I lost control. I was having difficulty getting straightened out. The car wanted to turn over. It was a strain for me to control it. I was crossing the lanes heading for the median on the expressway. "Lord please do not let me die here," was my cry. Then I noticed no cars were coming to hit me for I had already crossed three lanes of traffic and I hit the expressway wall. My eyes were closed when I crashed into the wall. Just as I opened my eyes and looked around, two young men were standing in the road looking at me. I beckoned to them and they came to me.

"Please help me out of the car." As they started toward me, the car began to smoke, and they pulled back. Then I said, "Lord, please do not let me see myself burn to death," and the smoke stopped. The young men came and pulled me out of my car, and sat me down on the expressway.

In no time I felt severe pain in my left side. When I tried to take a breath, I could not breathe. I was not getting enough air. I felt bones sticking into my chest. When I put my left arm down to my side, my bones stuck me. I asked one of the young men to lean my back against his knees so I could breathe and for him to hold my left arm out, away from my body, so my bones do not puncture my heart. The young man did what I asked without saying a word. How he did it, I cannot understand. I felt it must have been difficult for him as he was bending over me and holding out my heavy left arm. You see, I must admit, my arms are pretty heavy. However, the young man never complained or said a word as he held up my left arm. I strongly felt that he was an angel sent from God. I kept praying to God, asking Him not to let me die there on the expressway. "Please God, keep me conscious from fainting," I pleaded.

Suddenly, I saw darkness fall before my eyes. Slowly the darkness was going down to the ground until it touched the asphalt. I then began saying to myself, "I am losing my sight." Therefore, I prayed again, "Lord please do not let me lose consciousness." For a moment, I thought I was fainting. The darkness was so thick you could not see through it. I could see the line of the darkness as it was going up. It had an edge like a straight line. It was like an object in front of me. Just as it had come down it lifted slowly and I could see the sun just as brightly as it was shining before. I don't know how long the darkness stayed, but as it lifted I realized I was seeing something supernatural and magnificent! My thoughts began to wander until He stopped me with a touch.

I heard the other young man say, "Rescue is here!" The sun was shining brightly as it had before. No clouds were in the sky. Rescue took me to Jackson Memorial Hospital Trauma Unit. On my way to the hospital, the trip was extremely painful. I told the EMT how painful it was to breathe and they laughed at me. The violent jerking of the ambulance made the pain even more unbearable than it already was.

Then the questions came when I said, "My ribs are broken." They took X-rays and said I had no fractures at all. I prayed again, "Lord, please let them see that my ribs are broken." They saw the pneumothorax in my lung and the doctor tried to stick a tube in my lung to drain it. After 3 stabs, he realized my ribs were broken. Once he saw what came out of the tube—blood, water, and bubbles—he took me to the scanner. They medicated me and I was asleep before I knew it.

When I awoke, the doctor stood by me with a terrible look on his face and in his eyes. "Lady you are going to die," he said. He was looking at me in shock. They were confused by my level of alertness considering how damaged my body was, especially my internal organs. How could I be so alert and able to tell them exactly what was wrong with me? I wasn't even supposed to be conscious, much less alive. But I knew God had come to the scene and kept me alive so I could tell them why I was having difficulty breathing. I was gasping for air using only my right lung.

The Morning Before the Day I should Have Died

Because of my medical training as a nurse, I was able to diagnose a failing lung. How could they not see via X-ray that the left side of my rib cage was smaller than the right? My ribs were pushed in. He clasped his ten fingers together and said, "Lady your ribs are like this. You cannot live with them like that or you will *die!* But thank God we have perfected a process to fix your ribs if you want me to fix them," the doctor said. I asked, "*If* I want you to?"

He said they would have to rush me to surgery to prevent my ribs from starting to heal in that position. The long process began. During this time, I had many visits from my co-workers who worked in medical records with me. They saw my poor physical condition and realized how deadly my accident really could have been. Through their visits, I was encouraged and believed that God would see me through.

Members from my church, including the choir and the pastor, all visited with me. They prayed with me. They sang with me. They encouraged me to hold on. The doctors got me ready for surgery on Saturday morning. I went to surgery and my God was with me. Sunday morning when I awoke, I was in the intensive care unit of the hospital. I could breathe with no pain. I looked around and was relieved I was still alive. I was able to breathe deeply with no pain.

In my thoughts, I asked, *was it God that came to me in the thick cloud?* Suddenly, I felt a slap of four fingers on my forehead and heard a voice that was clear and calm. The voice spoke loudly in my ears, "Don't you see I came? And I let you see me?" I screamed, "Oh my God!" He touched me oh he touched me and oh the joy that flooded my soul!

I felt I was in the presence of the Almighty God. At that moment, tears flowed down my face. For the first time since the accident, I cried tears. I was terrified but elated. God the Almighty had come down from heaven to rescue me and save my life. For a sinner like me, he left his throne to save me. He also sent two young men as angels to keep me from getting hit by a car a second time. I was dying and God answered my plea. What a God we serve! I love the Lord, He heard my cry.

He wants me to tell the world that He cares about us and He hears us when we call on Him. He is the same God that came to the Israelites in the thick cloud, and to Moses on Mount Sinai. Read Exodus 40 verses 34 and 38. He is the same God who was in the temple and in the wilderness. He comes to man today. Just trust Him and call on Him.

I get to tell the world what He did for me. For what he did for me, He will do for you too. However, you must develop a relationship with Him. As a sinner, His blood and love cover me daily from the Evil One. I have had cancer twice, yet He kept me alive so I could tell my story.

When I got ready to tell my story, I spoke to a reporter at Trinity Broadcasting Network (TBN). His advice was for me to tell my story through TBN. Before giving me an appointment time, Jenn Crouch, the owner of TBN, passed away. Her death was a shock to me and my co-workers. TBN employees Matt and Lowry sent me a letter. The letter stated that I now needed to meet with them to discuss my story before going on TBN. I sent them a short note about my experience. I told them I needed to tell the whole world about my miraculous encounter with God. I hoped they would introduce it on their program. Well, you see that was easier said than done. I did not have the money to write the book as they suggested to me.

My accident case took five years before it went to court. My lawyer would not allow me to communicate with the person who drove the Mack truck that struck me on the I-95 expressway.

After I went to the hospital in the ambulance, the police officer that came to the scene did not take the name of the two young men who helped to save my life that day. What a blessing it would have been to receive the names and numbers of the two young men who came to my rescue on the day of my accident.

While in the hospital, the police officer came to get my statement about the accident. I was sure he would have their names and their information to give to me so I could get in touch with the young men. I wanted to thank them for being my guardian angels. They helped block traffic from hitting my car after I crossed three lanes in heavy rush hour traffic. I am sure the Lord put it in them to block traffic with their truck to save me from being hit a second time. The officer stated he was busy with another accident and did not see the point of taking their names because they said they did not see when the truck hit my car. Even when they did so much for me it did not cross his mind that I would want to know who they were so I could thank them.

I was dissatisfied with the officer's service. How could I get in touch with those young men? My prayer and hopes are that God will allow me to meet them one day so I can thank them personally. I never heard their names mentioned even when they spoke to the driver in Spanish and English. I do know that they were of Latin descent. I was gasping for air to breathe during the time they were with me.

Therefore, I was unable to engage in conversation with them. I could only pray to God. I wanted my God to keep me from losing consciousness and keep me alive. And He did.

May you find inspiration in reading the following scriptures as I did.

Exodus 4:10-11

Numbers 11:12, 24-25

Numbers 12:5-16

Genesis 32:30-32

My Life As A Child

I made up my mind to serve the Lord when I was a child. I believe I was about five years old. I would be following in the footsteps of my parents and learning all about the Lord just as they had taught me, and my grandparents had taught them. God had become a friend to talk to whenever I felt alone. By the time I was able to read, my Bible was the book I gravitated to the most. I learned to pronounce syllables, which helped me to be able to read just about any book I came across. My schooling was enhanced by much Bible study as a child. I spent a lot of time studying with my dad.

Growing up I was teased by my siblings and the result was a feeling of loneliness. I learned early to confide in my unseen friend, Jesus Christ. Although I couldn't see Him, I could talk to Him and call Him by name. He knew my name.

I was brought up in the Seventh-Day Adventist Church from the age of seven. While attending church, I grew closer to God. We had Bible study every morning. Singing and worship were a must. By studying His Word and learning to memorize verses and whole chapters, I could recite whole chapters of scripture by memory. Family Bible study was routine in our household. My father often prayed to God for the protection of his family day and night.

My father became an Elder in the church even when he could not read well. But in those days, that didn't matter much. Our family was active in the church. Mommy was a church clerk. Me and my four other sisters became a choir. We were the quintet singers. Daddy had an excellent memory and could speak well so his sermons were always dynamic and won many souls over to God. The church grew immensely after we became members. Later, he became Leader of the church, which meant he'd be required to speak more often.

370   I've Found a Friend

JAMES G. SMALL   GEORGE C. STEBBINS

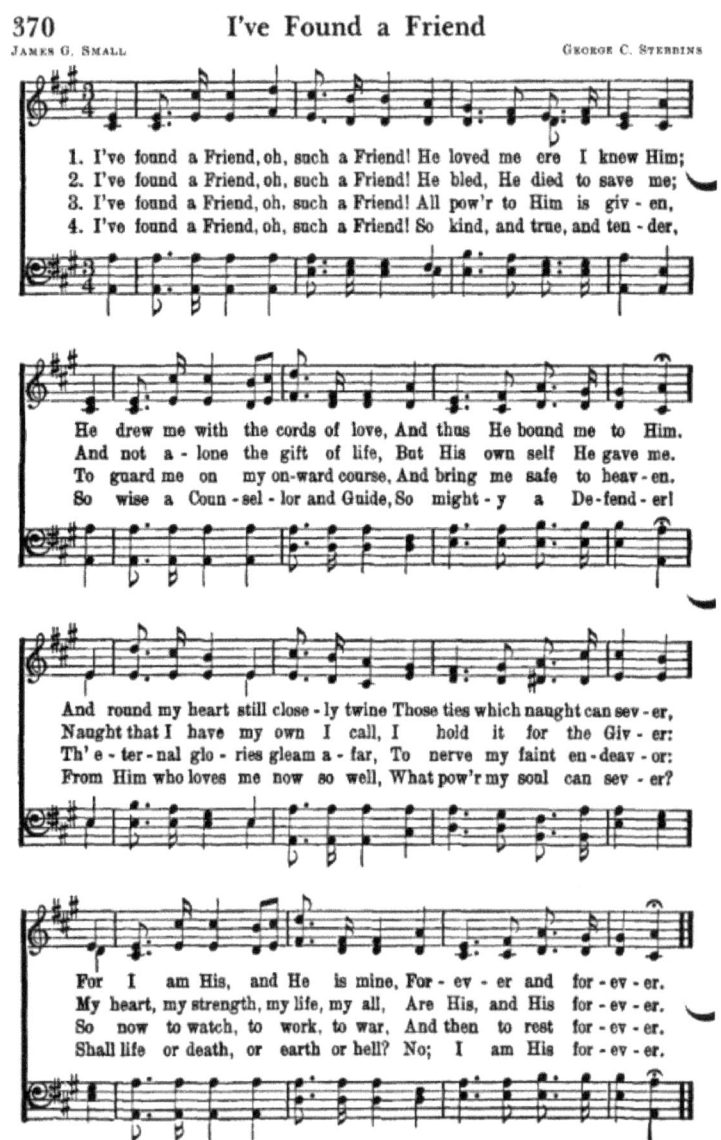

1. I've found a Friend, oh, such a Friend! He loved me ere I knew Him;
2. I've found a Friend, oh, such a Friend! He bled, He died to save me;
3. I've found a Friend, oh, such a Friend! All pow'r to Him is giv - en,
4. I've found a Friend, oh, such a Friend! So kind, and true, and ten - der,

He drew me with the cords of love, And thus He bound me to Him.
And not a - lone the gift of life, But His own self He gave me.
To guard me on my on-ward course, And bring me safe to heav - en.
So wise a Coun - sel - lor and Guide, So might - y a De - fend - er!

And round my heart still close - ly twine Those ties which naught can sev - er,
Naught that I have my own I call, I hold it for the Giv - er:
Th' e - ter - nal glo - ries gleam a - far, To nerve my faint en - deav - or:
From Him who loves me now so well, What pow'r my soul can sev - er?

For I am His, and He is mine, For - ev - er and for - ev - er.
My heart, my strength, my life, my all, Are His, and His for - ev - er.
So now to watch, to work, to war, And then to rest for - ev - er.
Shall life or death, or earth or hell? No; I am His for - ev - er.

Whenever I heard daddy fumbling with the Bible, searching for verses, I would offer to help him by finding the scripture reading as fast as he had mentioned it. This made learning my Bible inevitable. I learned the books of the Bible and their locations with ease, and daddy was able to speak freely. Finding scripture would later create competition among my sisters and I. Whoever found the verse and stood up to read first for daddy was the winner.

Now daddy could see he had real help. I became his Bible worker on Sundays when I should have been playing with my friends. He always wanted me to conduct Bible study. I started losing my enthusiasm and it wasn't fun anymore. But little did I know, Bible study was a blessing in disguise. The Lord used it to get me closer to Him and I am thankful. It was an absolute pleasure to be able to walk and talk with my daddy and to see and meet people that I otherwise might not have. I felt proud when people accepted the Lord as their savior. I was being trained to be a Bible worker early in life.

I was baptized at age ten and my life has never been the same. God became my closest friend throughout my teenage years and my adult life. I left home and went to college, and in the process learned to really trust and rely on God. When my daddy then decided to leave our home in Jamaica and travel to London, England to be with my older sisters who were training to be nurses, my life would change again. I was forced to leave school and return home to be with my baby sister until she could take and pass her exams to receive her Senior Cambridge degree. My mother had to leave for England to assist my Father with the expenses. Room and board were consuming all of his money so he needed my mother there.

I planned to return to school once my sister had passed her exams. Before long, I was able to send her to England with my parents to continue her education. My life, on the other hand, took a dramatic change. I was raped in my sleep by a friend I trusted. I became a mother and my life seemed to have been derailed. I never went back to college as I had hoped. Before I knew it, I was a mother of two sons and my life was hard.

In the midst of it all, God was there for me. He never left me, and I trusted Him to help me through. Just when I thought my life was a disastrous mess, the opportunity came for me to travel to America. There, I'd be able to get back into school and complete my education to become a nurse. That was a promise I made to my grandmother as I watched her struggle and then die five days after having a stroke. Back then doctors were not equipped to handle stroke patients. It took me months to complete a course in Home Economics and Domestic Science from Beaumont Comprehensive College. I also took a nursing course from St. Johns Ambulance association where I obtained a certificate.

Imagine the anxiety I went through. Leaving my home, the place where I had family and a few friends. But even more heartbreaking I'd be leaving behind two babies under the age of three. My parents were in England and I was planning to go to America, where I had no one and knew no one. I was sponsored to take care of a disabled girl. I had to obtain a visa to be able to work in the U.S. How do you leave your kids behind and just go away? I placed them in the hands of God, my one, true friend. He kept me alive through much and I knew He would never leave them or me. Jesus Jesus Jesus! The time came for me to travel to the U.S.

I kept my visa for three months until the day before it would expire. When I arrived at the airport in Jamaica I saw a souvenir that read, "God grant me the serenity to accept the things I cannot change, courage to change the things I can, and wisdom to know the difference." It answered my prayer. So I bought it and it served as my motto. It was my mission. I took the plane to Miami to meet the people who sponsored me, Mr. and Mrs. Ziger. When I arrived there,

140 I Want Jesus to Walk with Me

1 I want Je - sus to walk with me;
2 In my tri - als, Lord, walk with me;
3 When I'm in trou - ble, Lord, walk with me;

I want Je - sus to walk with me;
in my tri - als, Lord, walk with me;
when I'm in trou - ble, Lord, walk with me;

all a - long my pil - grim jour - ney,
when my heart is al - most break - ing,
when my head is bowed in sor - row,

Lord, I want Je - sus to walk with me.
Lord, I want Je - sus to walk with me.
Lord, I want Je - sus to walk with me.

Words: African American spiritual
Music (SOJOURNER irregular): African American spiritual, P.D.

they had been waiting for me. Originally, they had hired a young lady named Francine to work until I could arrive, which led to her losing her job. They returned to Long Island, New York where they lived. I took the long ride on a Greyhound bus to Newark. Then a train to Long Island. A beautiful place.

Imagine what was going on in the minds of everyone involved; my sponsor, Francine, and of course me. God was in disguise, working out the plans for everyone in this story. When I met Francine, I thought she was a lovely young lady. She needed the job and had gotten used to working with the family. I fell in love with her personality and the person she was during the week I spent there. The Ziger's could not afford to pay both of us. Even when there was no work, I would be there anyway for their daughter. She was mentally disabled and required constant care. What about me and my two children in Jamaica? What was happening to them there? Were they crying and looking for me to come home to them? It was time for me to make a change. It was time for me to muster up some courage. This would ultimately become my best choice.

I told Francine if she wanted the job, she could have it. I would rather go back to Miami where the weather was warm and reminiscent of Jamaica. And besides, I'd be just that much closer to my own kids. She was so relieved to hear that. We had worked all day that day. We did holiday cleaning. The basement had been locked up for years. Supposedly, they had a party some time back and it hadn't been cleaned since. I remember Mr. Ziger telling us to take the day off. But Mrs. Ziger wouldn't have it. She wanted that basement cleaned even if it took all day. Well, Francine and I didn't get done until just as the Ziger's were arriving back home for the day.

It was a different kind of day for both of us. We were so tired, dragging our bodies up the steps with mop and broom in tow. We were dirty and starving from cleaning all day with no break. I mean, we cleaned

1 I know not why God's won-drous grace to   me   he has   made known,
2 I know not how this   sav - ing faith to   me   he did   im - part,
3 I know not how the   Spir - it moves, con - vinc - ing us   of   sin,
4 I know not what of   good or   ill may   be   re - served for   me.

nor why, un-wor-thy, Christ in love   re - deemed me   for his   own.
nor how be-liev - ing   in   his Word wrought peace with-in   my   heart.
re - veal-ing Je - sus through the Word,   cre - at - ing faith in   him.
of   wea - ry ways or   gold - en days,   be - fore his face I   see.

Refrain

But "I   know whom I have be - liev - ed, and am per-suad - ed   that he   is

a - ble to keep that which I've com - mit-ted un - to him a-gainst that day."

Text: Daniel W. Whittle, 1883, based on 2 Timothy 1:12
Tune: James McGranahan, 1883

CM with refrain
EL NATHAN

old cobwebs, dust storms, and garbage that had accumulated over what seemed like years. Their car drove into the garage just as we came up. Francine had to rush off to the shower so she could begin to prepare dinner. And I scurried off to their daughter to assist her in the bathroom. I desperately needed to use it too, but she took priority. I was not allowed to shower and change like Francine. I had to tend to the Zigers' daughter.

After about two hours Mrs. Ziger came and looked at me with disgust and asked if I had taken a bath since I had been there. That sent me crying, running upstairs. I showered, got dressed, and refused to come back down for the evening. That night Mr. Ziger came to me privately and asked if I wanted to leave. He said it was okay with him and apologized for how his wife behaved earlier. She robbed us of our day off when he clearly said we didn't have to work. It was the 4th of July. It was a holiday.

"I know not why God's wondrous love to me He hath made known" (*I Know Not Why God's Wondrous Grace, D.W. Whittle*).

I thanked him for sponsoring me and for allowing me to have work and be able to go to school. But I told him Francine needed the job more than I did. I could go and work with someone else and would rather be in Miami anyway. He said he was releasing me of my contract to work. A contract that technically bound my services to their family for two years. He said he would call the agency that I was with and help me find another job taking care of another little girl in Miami Beach.

Six months later, I was on my own again; free to work as I pleased and for whom I pleased. God was always in control of my life. I could have never predicted things would have turned out the way that they did. "God grant me the serenity to accept the things I cannot change, courage to change the things I can, and wisdom to know the difference."

641 Higher Ground

THE CHURCH ON MISSION

1. I'm press-ing on the up-ward way, new heights I'm gain-ing ev-ery day; still pray-ing as I on-ward bound, "Lord, plant my feet on high-er ground."

2. My heart has no de-sire to stay where doubts a-rise and fears dis-may; though some may dwell where these a-bound, my prayer, my aim is high-er ground.

3. I want to live a-bove the world, though Sa-tan's darts at me are hurled; for faith has caught the joy-ful sound, the song of saints on high-er ground.

4. I want to scale the ut-most height and catch a gleam of glo-ry bright; but still I'll pray till heaven I've found, "Lord, lead me on to high-er ground."

Lord, lift me up and let me stand, by faith, on heav-en's ta-ble-land, a high-er plane than I have found; Lord, plant my feet on high-er ground.

WORDS: Johnson Oatman, Jr., 1892
MUSIC: Charles H. Gabriel, 1892

HIGHER GROUND
LM with refrain

I was free to get a job at night as a Nurse's Aid at Mount Sinai Hospital. And by day I was attending school to get my high school diploma. From there to Lindsey Hopkins for my nursing certificate as an LPN, and then on to Miami Dade for my Associate of Arts degree. God was always there helping me while I was working, going to school, and raising a family of now three boys alone. Oh but God!

"I'm pressing on the upward way" (*Higher Ground*, Johnson Oatman, Jr.).

Reflection Summary: Why Me?

Allow me to go back to the year 2009, when I had the accident. There I was in the presence of the Almighty God. How was I to act? How would you act? Would you jump up and shout? Would you scream for joy? I could have but I did not because I could not. My body was injured by my accident. Put yourself in my position for a minute. You are in the presence of the Creator of this world, our Divine Savior, our Holy and Righteous God. All I could do was pray, pray, and pray some more. And that's just what I did. My prayers were comforting to my soul.

I am a sinner who deserves to die in His presence and especially after I saw Him. But for some reason, I am still alive to tell my story about seeing Jesus.

Whenever I think about that day, I get chills knowing that I am still alive. "Why did He come to save me from dying?" I ask myself that question nearly every day. *Why me?* I am no different from anyone else on this earth that got into a car accident and died at the scene. Why did He respond so quickly to my pleading cry? All I know is that Jesus loves me so much.

Why did He hear my prayers? Why did He respond urgently to my accident by sending two young men, Angels, to protect me from being hit a second time by oncoming traffic? You see, I veered across three lanes on a busy expressway. Yes, He did hear and answer my prayers when I knew I was about to die. I was hurting and gasping for air. God knew how painful my situation was because He had experienced pain on the cross of Calvary. The cross is where He died to save you and me and anyone else who calls on Him.

Remember the thief on the cross? He told Jesus, "Remember me when thou comest into thy kingdom." Yes, that one. What did Jesus do? Jesus stopped dying and spoke to the thief. What did Jesus say? "Verily I say unto thee, Today shalt thou be with me in paradise" (Luke 23:42-43, KJV).

You have heard the sermon preached often. The story is a love story. It tells how much the Lord cares about mankind. He left heaven and came and died a cruel and shameful death for mankind. He did it so you and I could be saved from eternal death. He wants us to have life everlasting. Acknowledge Jesus as your Lord and Savior. Develop a relationship with Him daily.

The Gospel is about Jesus Christ. You see, Jesus promised in His Gospel never to leave us nor to forsake us through our trials, pains, and sufferings. Believe me, I suffered from my car accident. On occasion, I tried to take a breath of air and I could not because I was having excruciating pain. I gasped for air with no knowledge of the damages that were inside my body. My internal damages could not be seen by the naked eye. My legs were injured and bleeding. But it was obvious that inside my body I was severely injured. I had ruptured my spleen and lung, and had broken bones that no one could have imagined.

The Gospel Commission that Jesus left for us as disciples is, "Go ye therefore, and teach all nations, baptizing them in the name of the Father, and of the Son, and of the Holy Ghost: Teaching them to observe all things whatsoever I have commanded you: and, lo, I am with you always, even unto the end of the world. Amen" (Matthew 28:19-20, KJV).

You see, I started talking to the Lord as a child. Crying to Him when my sisters mistreated me or said mean words to me. When I complained to my parents, I did not get a good response from them, so who did I turn to? The Lord! I could explain my side to Him and He would listen to me without questioning me or laughing at me. When I would ask Him for an answer about something, I would go to my Bible and open it at random. There in my opened Bible, I would earnestly read the pages and find answers to my questions.

Often, I would recall information I read from the Bible and know that the answer came directly to me from God. This practice is one that I have lived by throughout my life.

When I became an adult, I found it most important to talk to God about everything from raising my children to making health and business decisions. God has been my counselor and He has never failed me. In sickness, I would call on Him and He would carry me in His arms and on His shoulders. Throughout my knee surgeries, I lost my job and had no help. He was there to instruct me as to what to do. For one year and seven months, I was out of work. He gave me back my former job. But soon after that, I was without work again for another nine months because I was sick and in pain with cancer. Guess what? He provided for me then, and God eventually brought me back to that job, while I was undergoing chemotherapy treatments for breast cancer.

Every day when I went to the hospital, I was never alone. Jesus was with me. On many days, I was so weak and helpless with no family to lean on. But His strength carried me every step of the way. I would say, "God's strength is sufficient." I prayed often, I turned to Jesus, and He would see me through. He never left me, and I was determined to stay with Him.

I had breast cancer and received four months of chemotherapy treatment. After having my left breast removed I sustained third-degree burns from radiation to my chest and dealt with the burns alone. However, Jesus was there with me. I had God. I never lost my faith in Him. By praying daily and depending on Him for help, He saw me through my difficult times. I can tell the world, "What He has done for me, He will do for you; if only you would trust Him."

When you have no idea how your day will end or what happens next, *trust* Jesus. Be like *Job*.

Though He slay me, yet I will trust Him.

Job 13:15, KJV

Thick clouds are covering for him, that he seath not; and he walketh in the circuit of heaven.

Job 22:14, KJV

For I know that my Redeemer liveth, and that he shall stand at the latter day upon earth: And though after my death worms destroy this body, yet in my flesh still I will see God: Whom I shall see for myself, and mine eyes shall behold, and not another; though my veins be consumed within me.

Job 19: 25-27 KJV

He hath put my brethren far from me, and mine acquaintance are verily estranged from me. My kinsfolk has failed, and my familiar friends have forgotten me.

Job 19:13-14, KJV

When my breast was leaking from chemo I felt deserted because family and friends stayed away from me.

Oh, that my words were now written! Oh that they were printed in a book! That they were graven with an iron pen and lead in the rock for ever! For I know that my Redeemer liveth, and that He shall stand at the latter day upon the earth.

Job 23-25, KJV

The Holy Spirit is God in the spirit. He can move through the air as the wind blows across your face. It moves you and makes you feel His presence.

Likewise, it travels into your heart and soul and makes you think that there is a God to love and worship. It makes you want to sing, dance, and rejoice that there is a God who cares for you and helps you when you're down. He comforts you with things from nature like flowers, water, sun, and trees, that we can smell, see, and touch. We can taste wonderful fruits and food. When you are sad, He can make you glad with His comforting words. When you are sick, He can heal and comfort you. He will give you rest and sleep. The Holy Spirit consoles you and helps you pray to God for strength to overcome the Evil One. Hope in God that tomorrow will be better. We live with this promise from God. He will be with you always.

God in His matchless love saw me across three lanes on the I-95 expressway without dying. He put kindness and a caring heart within one of the young men. That young man saw the possible danger of cars hitting my car. He stopped the oncoming traffic to prevent multiple car collisions and he kept other people from being killed or hurt that day. Daily, people would see and hear about car accidents on television, in the community, and on the news. Sometimes a single car accident would cause a chain reaction wherein many people would get hurt or lose their lives. People get hurt on roadways due to drivers' carelessness or inattentiveness. Only God spared my life, and I kindly thanked Him.

God in His goodness heard my cry and put a plan into action to save me. He sent two angels to protect me from being crushed that day. But that was not the end. The devil wanted to kill me by crushing my ribs; even though I never received a bad injury on the outside of my body. When I thought I was dying, God heard me struggling to breathe. That must have been what it felt like for Jesus on the cross when He took the beatings, shame, and pains for our sins.

Remember when He was dying on the cross for our sins? He had to pull up on His nail-pierced hands and feet to take a breath of air. And with his weight bearing down on His lungs, breathing was difficult for Him.

On the day of my accident, Jesus knew what I was feeling. He knew how painful it was to get a breath of air. I would have to pull those jammed ribs from inside of each other. This was very similar to the folding of my fingers together. My left lung was punctured. It was as if air was being squeezed out. Yet, instead, my lungs were being filled with fluids.

Jesus came in a thick cloud to save me. Think of Jesus watching the scene from above and knowing that although He had sent two Angels to keep me from being crushed, He knew I was going to die there that day. He put aside caring for the world to care for me. Like the Shepherd who led ninety-nine sheep into the wilderness, Jesus stopped what He was doing to go in search of that one lost sheep and bring it back to the fold. Heaven rejoices when even one sinner is saved. I was that one sinner. I was dying so I called out to Jesus, "Lord, please do no let me die right here." He heard me from heaven and came to my rescue. He heard my moans and groans. My petition reached His throne. For as long as I live and troubles come, I'll hasten to His throne. I love the Lord. He heard my cry.

Imagine the Savior coming down in a thick cloud as He travels to come to receive His chosen people. A thick cloud will cover His magnificent appearance. What a great day that will be! Thank you, Lord, for coming soon to receive and save a sinner like me!

DREAM

I was reminded through a dream years after my accident that I had been commissioned by God to write this book. I had started once before but now it is clearer than ever it must be accomplished.

I had a dream of caring for a lady who had out-lived all of her family. She was so beautiful and had skin so soft and smooth it was like velvet; no wrinkles or scars. She was smart, intelligent, and showed no signs of aging or ailment. As I spoke with her, I laughed about myself. *Will I be like her if I live to be ten years older?* In the dream, as I was thinking my day was over the peculiar lady who I thought had gone to bed called to me. She asked me to come and take my things. She wasn't in bed and asleep as I had believed. I walked into the room where she was. It was a sewing room and she had numerous pieces of fabric and material scattered all about preparing to make garments. Linen and clothing lined the room. She was showing me her unfinished work. I am a dress-maker myself with ample unfinished work and materials. Jesus always knows how to speak to me through my dreams.

When I woke up and realized it was a dream, I stopped and thanked Him. I asked the Lord to show me what to write in this book. I didn't know how to explain what I had witnessed. All I knew was that He showed Himself to me in the clouds just as He did for the Hebrew children. He directed me to the book of Hebrews, Chapter 7, and I found all the proof I needed from Genesis to Revelation that attests that Jesus is the name of God that came to Moses in the thickness of the clouds, as well as the children of the Israelites, and all throughout the Bible.

He's the same God that died on the cross to save mankind. He's the same God that answers our prayers. Everyone who has faith in God and believes in the Messiah is sure to have their prayers answered.

And everyone who has a personal relationship with Him and believes that by faith He is Jesus ascended and soon to return, it is for them that Jesus comes again to take and collect their new heavenly home.

I believe this dream was the Lord's way of telling me to finish this book before I get too old. Thank you, Lord, for your patience and guidance. I will get *Your* word out to the world that all may know that You sit high and look low. God hears the cries of His children, in joy, sorrow, and suffering. And He comes to their aid as He has and continues to do for me.

Hebrews Chapter 7

New King James Version

The King of Righteousness

For this Melchizedek, king of Salem, priest of the Most High God, who met Abraham returning from the slaughter of the kings and blessed him, to whom also Abraham gave a tenth part of all, first being translated "king of righteousness," and then also king of Salem, meaning "king of peace," without father, without mother, without genealogy, having neither beginning of days nor end of life, but made like the Son of God, remains a priest continually.

Now consider how great this man was, to whom even the patriarch Abraham gave a tenth of the spoils. And indeed those who are of the sons of Levi, who receive the priesthood, have a commandment to receive tithes from the people according to the law, that is, from their brethren, though they have come from the loins of Abraham; but he whose genealogy is not derived from them received tithes from Abraham and blessed him who had the promises. Now beyond all contradiction the lesser is blessed by the better. Here mortal men receive tithes, but there he receives them, of whom it is witnessed that he lives. Even Levi, who receives tithes, paid tithes through Abraham, so to speak, one-tenth for he was still in the loins of his father when Melchizedek met him.

Need for a New Priesthood

Therefore, if perfection were through the Levitical priesthood (for under it the people received the law), what further need was there that another priest should rise according to the order of Melchizedek, and not be called according to the order of Aaron? For the priesthood being changed, of necessity there is also a change of the law. For He of whom these things are spoken belongs to another tribe, from which no man has officiated at the altar.

For it is evident that our Lord arose from Judah, of which tribe Moses spoke nothing concerning priesthood. And it is yet far more evident if, in the likeness of Melchizedek, there arises another priest who has come, not according to the law of a fleshly commandment, but according to the power of an endless life. For He testifies:

"You are a priest forever
According to the order of Melchizedek."

For on the one hand there is an annulling of the former commandment because of its weakness and unprofitableness, for the law made nothing perfect; on the other hand, there is the bringing in of a better hope, through which we draw near to God.

Greatness of the New Priest

And inasmuch as He was not made priest without an oath (for they have become priests without an oath, but He with an oath by Him who said to Him:

"The Lord has sworn
And will not relent,
'You are a priest forever
According to the order of Melchizedek'"),

by so much more Jesus has become a surety of a better covenant.

Also there were many priests, because they were prevented by death from continuing. But He, because He continues forever, has an unchangeable priesthood. Therefore He is also able to save to the uttermost those who come to God through Him, since He always lives to make intercession for them.

For such a High Priest was fitting for us, who is holy, harmless, undefiled, separate from sinners, and has become higher than the heavens; who does not need daily, as those high priests, to offer up sacrifices, first for His own sins and then for the people's, for this He did once for all when He offered up Himself. For the law appoints as high priests men who have weakness, but the word of the oath, which came after the law, appoints the Son who has been perfected forever.

Hebrews Chapter 8

The New Priestly Service

Now this is the main point of the things we are saying: We have such a High Priest, who is seated at the right hand of the throne of the Majesty in the heavens, a Minister of the sanctuary and of the true tabernacle which the Lord erected, and not man.

For every high priest is appointed to offer both gifts and sacrifices. Therefore it is necessary that this One also have something to offer. For if He were on earth, He would not be a priest, since there are priests who offer the gifts according to the law; who serve the copy and shadow of the heavenly things, as Moses was divinely instructed when he was about to make the tabernacle. For He said, "See that you make all things according to the pattern shown you on the mountain." But now He has obtained a more excellent ministry, inasmuch as He is also Mediator of a better covenant, which was established on better promises.

A New Covenant

For if that first covenant had been faultless, then no place would have been sought for a second. Because finding fault with them, He says: "Behold, the days are coming, says the Lord, when I will make a new covenant with the house of Israel and with the house of Judah—not according to the covenant that I made with their fathers in the day when I took them by the hand to lead them out of the land of Egypt; because they did not continue in My covenant, and I disregarded them, says the Lord. For this is the covenant that I will make with the house of Israel after those days, says the Lord: I will put My laws in their mind and write them on their hearts; and I will be their God, and they shall be My people. None of them shall teach his neighbor, and none his brother, saying, 'Know the Lord, for all shall know Me, from the least of them to the greatest of them. For I will be merciful to their unrighteousness, and their sins and their lawless deeds I will remember no more."

In that He says, "A new covenant," He has made the first obsolete. Now what is becoming obsolete and growing old is ready to vanish away.

Hebrews Chapter 9

The Earthly Sanctuary

Then indeed, even the first *covenant* had ordinances of divine service and the earthly sanctuary. For a tabernacle was prepared: the first *part*, in which *was* the lampstand, the table, and the showbread, which is called the sanctuary; and behind the second veil, the part of the tabernacle which is called the Holiest of All, which had the golden censer and the ark of the covenant overlaid on all sides with gold, in which *were* the golden pot that had the manna, Aaron's rod that budded, and the tablets of the covenant; and above it were the cherubim of glory overshadowing the mercy seat. Of these things we cannot now speak in detail.

Limitations of the Earthly Service

Now when these things had been thus prepared, the priests always went into the first part of the tabernacle, performing the services. But into the second part the high priest *went* alone once a year, not without blood, which he offered for himself and *for* the people's sins *committed* in ignorance; the Holy Spirit indicating this, that the way into the Holiest of All was not yet made manifest while the first tabernacle was still standing. It *was* symbolic for the present time in which both gifts and sacrifices are offered which cannot make him who performed the service perfect in regard to the conscience— *concerned* only with foods and drinks, various washings, and fleshly ordinances imposed until the time of reformation.

The Heavenly Sanctuary

But Christ came *as* High Priest of the good things to come, with the greater and more perfect tabernacle not made with hands, that is, not of this creation. Not with the blood of goats and calves, but with His own blood He entered the Most Holy Place once for all, having obtained eternal redemption. For if the blood of bulls and goats and the ashes of a heifer, sprinkling the unclean, sanctifies for the purifying of the flesh, how much more shall the blood of Christ, who through the eternal Spirit offered Himself without spot to God, cleanse your conscience from dead works to serve the living God? And for this reason He is the Mediator of the new covenant, by means of death, for the redemption of the transgressions under the first covenant, that those who are called may receive the promise of the eternal inheritance.

The Mediator's Death Necessary

For where there is a testament, there must also of necessity be the death of the testator. For a testament is in force after men are dead, since it has no power at all while the testator lives. Therefore not even the first *covenant* was dedicated without blood. For when Moses had spoken every precept to all the people according to the law, he took the blood of calves and goats, with water, scarlet wool, and hyssop, and sprinkled both the book itself and all the people, saying, "This *is* the blood of the covenant which God has commanded you." Then likewise he sprinkled with blood both the tabernacle and all the vessels of the ministry. And according to the law almost all things are purified with blood, and without shedding of blood there is no remission.

Greatness of Christ's Sacrifice

Therefore it *was* necessary that the copies of the things in the heavens should be purified with these, but the heavenly things themselves with better sacrifices than these. For Christ has not entered the holy places made with hands, *which* are copies of the true, but into heaven itself, now to appear in the presence of God for us; not that He should offer Himself often, as the high priest enters the Most Holy Place every year with blood of another—He then would have had to suffer often since the foundation of the world; but now, once at the end of the ages, He has appeared to put away sin by the sacrifice of Himself. And as it is appointed for men to die once, but after this the judgment, so Christ was offered once to bear the sins of many. To those who eagerly wait for Him He will appear a second time, apart from sin, for salvation.

Hebrews Chapter 10

Animal Sacrifices Insufficient

For the law, having a shadow of the good things to come, *and* not the very image of the things, can never with these same sacrifices, which they offer continually year by year, make those who approach perfect. For then would they not have ceased to be offered? For the worshipers, once purified, would have had no more consciousness of sins. But in those *sacrifices there is* a reminder of sins every year. For *it is* not possible that the blood of bulls and goats could take away sins.

Christ's Death Fulfills God's Will

Therefore, when He came into the world, He said:

"Sacrifice and offering You did not desire,
But a body You have prepared for Me.
In burnt offerings and *sacrifices* for sin
You had no pleasure.
Then I said, 'Behold, I have come—
In the volume of the book it is written of Me—
To do Your will, O God.'"

Previously saying, "Sacrifice and offering, burnt *offerings*, and offerings for sin You did not desire, nor had pleasure in *them*" (which are offered according to the law), then He said, "Behold, I have come to do Your will, O God." He takes away the first that He may establish the second. By that will we have been sanctified through the offering of the body of Jesus Christ once *for all*.

Christ's Death Perfects the Sanctified

And every priest stands ministering daily and offering repeatedly the same sacrifices, which can never take away sins. But this Man, after

He had offered one sacrifice for sins forever, sat down at the right hand of God, from that time waiting till His enemies are made His footstool. For by one offering He has perfected forever those who are being sanctified.

But the Holy Spirit also witnesses to us; for after He had said before,

"This is the covenant that I will make with them after those days, says the LORD: I will put My laws into their hearts, and in their minds I will write them," *then He adds*, "Their sins and their lawless deeds I will remember no more." Now where there is remission of these, *there is* no longer an offering for sin.

Hold Fast Your Confession

Therefore, brethren, having boldness to enter the Holiest by the blood of Jesus, by a new and living way which He consecrated for us, through the veil, that is, His flesh, and *having* a High Priest over the house of God, let us draw near with a true heart in full assurance of faith, having our hearts sprinkled from an evil conscience and our bodies washed with pure water. Let us hold fast the confession of *our* hope without wavering, for He who promised is faithful. And let us consider one another in order to stir up love and good works, not forsaking the assembling of ourselves together, as *is* the manner of some, but exhorting one *another*, and so much the more as you see the Day approaching.

The Just Live by Faith

For if we sin willfully after we have received the knowledge of the truth, there no longer remains a sacrifice for sins, but a certain fearful expectation of judgment, and fiery indignation which will devour the adversaries. Anyone who has rejected Moses' law dies without mercy on *the testimony of* two or three witnesses. Of how much worse punishment, do you suppose, will he be thought worthy who has trampled the Son of God underfoot, counted the blood of the covenant by which he was sanctified a common thing, and insulted the Spirit of grace? For we know Him who said, "Vengeance is Mine, I will repay," says the Lord. And again, "The LORD will judge His people." It is a fearful thing to fall into the hands of the living God.

But recall the former days in which, after you were illuminated, you endured a great struggle with sufferings: partly while you were made a spectacle both by reproaches and tribulations, and partly while you became companions of those who were so treated; for you had compassion on me in my chains, and joyfully accepted the plundering of your goods, knowing that you have a better and an enduring possession for yourselves in heaven. Therefore do not cast away your confidence, which has great reward. For you have need of endurance, so that after you have done the will of God, you may receive the promise:

"For yet a little while,
And He who is coming will come and will not tarry.
Now the just shall live by faith;
But if *anyone* draws back,
My soul has no pleasure in him."
But we are not of those who draw back to perdition, but of those who believe to the saving of the soul.

Hebrews Chapter 11

By Faith We Understand

Now faith is the substance of things hoped for, the evidence of things not seen. For by it the elders obtained a *good* testimony.

By faith we understand that the worlds were framed by the word of God, so that the things which are seen were not made of things which are visible.

Faith at the Dawn of History

By faith Abel offered to God a more excellent sacrifice than Cain, through which he obtained witness that he was righteous, God testifying of his gifts; and through it he being dead still speaks.

By faith Enoch was taken away so that he did not see death, "and was not found, because God had taken him"; for before he was taken he had this testimony, that he pleased God. But without faith *it is* impossible to please *Him*, for he who comes to God must believe that He is, and *that* He is a rewarder of those who diligently seek Him.

By faith Noah, being divinely warned of things not yet seen, moved with godly fear, prepared an ark for the saving of his household, by which he condemned the world and became heir of the righteousness which is according to faith.

Faithful Abraham

By faith Abraham obeyed when he was called to go out to the place which he would receive as an inheritance. And he went out, not knowing where he was going. By faith he dwelt in the land of promise as *in* a foreign country, dwelling in tents with Isaac and Jacob, the heirs with him of the same promise; for he waited for the city which has foundations, whose builder and maker *is* God.

By faith Sarah herself also received strength to conceive seed, and she bore a child when she was past the age, because she judged Him faithful who had promised. Therefore from one man, and him as good as dead, were born *as many* as the stars of the sky in multitude—innumerable as the sand which is by the seashore.

The Heavenly Hope

These all died in faith, not having received the promises, but having seen them afar off were assured of them, embraced *them* and confessed that they were strangers and pilgrims on the earth. For those who say such things declare plainly that they seek a homeland. And truly if they had called to mind that *country* from which they had come out, they would have had opportunity to return. But now they desire a better, that is, a heavenly *country*. Therefore God is not ashamed to be called their God, for He has prepared a city for them.

The Faith of the Patriarchs

By faith Abraham, when he was tested, offered up Isaac, and he who had received the promises offered up his only begotten *son*, of whom it was said, "In Isaac your seed shall be called," concluding that God was able to raise *him* up, even from the dead, from which he also received him in a figurative sense.

By faith Isaac blessed Jacob and Esau concerning things to come.

By faith Jacob, when he was dying, blessed each of the sons of Joseph, and worshiped, *leaning* on the top of his staff.

By faith Joseph, when he was dying, made mention of the departure of the children of Israel, and gave instructions concerning his bones.

The Faith of Moses

By faith Moses, when he was born, was hidden three months by his parents, because they saw *he was* a beautiful child; and they were not afraid of the king's command.

By faith Moses, when he became of age, refused to be called the son of Pharaoh's daughter, choosing rather to suffer affliction with the people of God than to enjoy the passing pleasures of sin, esteeming the reproach of Christ greater riches than the treasures in Egypt; for he looked to the reward.

By faith he forsook Egypt, not fearing the wrath of the king; for he endured as seeing Him who is invisible. By faith he kept the Passover and the sprinkling of blood, lest he who destroyed the firstborn should touch them.

By faith they passed through the Red Sea as by dry *land, whereas* the Egyptians, attempting to do so, were drowned.

By Faith They Overcame

By faith the walls of Jericho fell down after they were encircled for seven days. By faith the harlot Rahab did not perish with those who did not believe, when she had received the spies with peace.

And what more shall I say? For the time would fail me to tell of Gideon and Barak and Samson and Jephthah, also *of* David and Samuel and the prophets: who through faith subdued kingdoms, worked righteousness, obtained promises, stopped the mouths of lions, quenched the violence of fire, escaped the edge of the sword, out of weakness were made strong, became valiant in battle, turned to flight the armies of the aliens. Women received their dead raised to life again.

Others were tortured, not accepting deliverance, that they might obtain a better resurrection. Still others had trial of mockings and scourgings, yes, and of chains and imprisonment. They were stoned, they were sawn in two, were tempted, were slain with the sword. They wandered about in sheepskins and goatskins, being destitute, afflicted, tormented—of whom the world was not worthy. They wandered in deserts and mountains, *in* dens and caves of the earth.

And all these, having obtained a good testimony through faith, did not receive the promise, God having provided something better for us, that they should not be made perfect apart from us.

Hebrews Chapter 12

The Race of Faith

Therefore we also, since we are surrounded by so great a cloud of witnesses, let us lay aside every weight, and the sin which so easily ensnares *us*, and let us run with endurance the race that is set before us, looking unto Jesus, the author and finisher of *our* faith, who for the joy that was set before Him endured the cross, despising the shame, and has sat down at the right hand of the throne of God.

The Discipline of God

For consider Him who endured such hostility from sinners against Himself, lest you become weary and discouraged in your souls. You have not yet resisted to bloodshed, striving against sin. And you have forgotten the exhortation which speaks to you as to sons:

"My son, do not despise the chastening of the LORD,
Nor be discouraged when you are rebuked by Him;
For whom the LORD loves He chastens,
And scourges every son whom He receives."

If you endure chastening, God deals with you as with sons; for what son is there whom a father does not chasten? But if you are without chastening, of which all have become partakers, then you are illegitimate and not sons. Furthermore, we have had human fathers who corrected *us*, and we paid *them* respect. Shall we not much more readily be in subjection to the Father of spirits and live? For they indeed for a few days chastened us as seemed *best* to them, but He for *our* profit, that *we* may be partakers of His holiness. Now no chastening seems to be joyful for the present, but painful; nevertheless, afterward it yields the peaceable fruit of righteousness to those who have been trained by it.

Renew Your Spiritual Vitality

Therefore strengthen the hands which hang down, and the feeble knees, and make straight paths for your feet, so that what is lame may not be dislocated, but rather be healed.

Pursue peace with all *people*, and holiness, without which no one will see the Lord: looking carefully lest anyone fall short of the grace of God; lest any root of bitterness springing up cause trouble, and by this many become defiled; lest there be any fornicator or profane person like Esau, who for one morsel of food sold his birthright. For you know that afterward, when he wanted to inherit the blessing, he was rejected, for he found no place for repentance, though he sought it diligently with tears.

The Glorious Company

For you have not come to the mountain that may be touched and that burned with fire, and to blackness and darkness and tempest, and the sound of a trumpet and the voice of words, so that those who heard *it* begged that the word should not be spoken to them anymore. (For they could not endure what was commanded: "And if so much as a beast touches the mountain, it shall be stoned or shot with an arrow." And so terrifying was the sight *that* Moses said, "I am exceedingly afraid and trembling.")

But you have come to Mount Zion and to the city of the living God, the heavenly Jerusalem, to an innumerable company of angels, to the general assembly and church of the firstborn *who are* registered in heaven, to God the Judge of all, to the spirits of just men made perfect, to Jesus the Mediator of the new covenant, and to the blood of sprinkling that speaks better things than *that* of Abel.

Hear the Heavenly Voice

See that you do not refuse Him who speaks. For if they did not escape who refused Him who spoke on earth, much more *shall we not escape* if we turn away from Him who *speaks* from heaven, whose voice then shook the earth; but now He has promised, saying, "Yet once more I shake not only the earth, but also heaven." Now this, "Yet once more," indicates the removal of those things that are being shaken, as of things that are made, that the things which cannot be shaken may remain.

Therefore, since we are receiving a kingdom which cannot be shaken, let us have grace, by which we may serve God acceptably with reverence and godly fear. For our God *is* a consuming fire.

Hebrews Chapter 13

Concluding Moral Directions

Let brotherly love continue. Do not forget to entertain strangers, for by so *doing* some have unwittingly entertained angels. Remember the prisoners as if chained with them—those who are mistreated—since you yourselves are in the body also.

Marriage is honorable among all, and the bed undefiled; but fornicators and adulterers God will judge.

Let your conduct *be* without covetousness; *be* content with such things as you have. For He Himself has said, "I will never leave you nor forsake you." So we may boldly say:

"The LORD is my helper;
I will not fear.
What can man do to me?"

Concluding Religious Directions

Remember those who rule over you, who have spoken the word of God to you, whose faith follow, considering the outcome of *their* conduct. Jesus Christ *is* the same yesterday, today, and forever. Do not be carried about with various and strange doctrines. For *it is* good that the heart be established by grace, not with foods which have not profited those who have been occupied with them.

We have an altar from which those who serve the tabernacle have no right to eat. For the bodies of those animals, whose blood is brought into the sanctuary by the high priest for sin, are burned outside the camp. Therefore Jesus also, that He might sanctify the people with His own blood, suffered outside the gate. Therefore let us go forth to Him, outside the camp, bearing His reproach. For here we have no continuing city, but we seek the one to come. Therefore by Him let us continually offer the sacrifice of praise to God, that is, the fruit of *our* lips, giving thanks to His name. But do not forget to do good and to share, for with such sacrifices God is well pleased.

Obey those who rule over you, and be submissive, for they watch out for your souls, as those who must give account. Let them do so with joy and not with grief, for that would be unprofitable for you.

Prayer Requested

Pray for us; for we are confident that we have a good conscience, in all things desiring to live honorably. But I especially urge *you* to do this, that I may be restored to you the sooner.

Benediction, Final Exhortation, Farewell

Now may the God of peace who brought up our Lord Jesus from the dead, that great Shepherd of the sheep, through the blood of the everlasting covenant, make you complete in every good work to do His will, working in you what is well pleasing in His sight, through Jesus Christ, to whom *be* glory forever and ever. Amen.

And I appeal to you, brethren, bear with the word of exhortation, for I have written to you in few words. Know that *our* brother Timothy has been set free, with whom I shall see you if he comes shortly.

Greet all those who rule over you, and all the saints. Those from Italy greet you.

Grace *be* with you all. Amen.

My prayer is that everyone who reads this book will catch a glimpse of what I experienced in my life: trusting God and Him taking care of me and my family. Let this book be a reference for all women who are forced to leave behind their families and countries to earn a living that they may be able to provide for their families. God will care for you if you trust Him. Let Him lead your life and allow Him to see you through. His grace is sufficient (2 Corinthians 12:9).

My life as an adult was filled with ups and downs. I came to this country in 1967, during an era when there was much discrimination. Whenever I was job hunting, I would request to be off on Sabbaths and I was usually successful in getting what I asked for. Most of the time, it was easier when I agreed to work the night shift. The dreaded shift that no one wanted to work. In the medical field, I was able to have Fridays and Saturdays off, which made it easier for me to attend my church activities. Other co-workers wanted to be off on Sabbath but were afraid to ask for it when they were hired, and they became jealous of me.

The Evil One was not pleased to see me able to work and raise my kids going church every week and praising God. He created changes in scheduling that put me in situations where I had to ask to exchange days off with my co-workers. Changes in management, over time, forced me to work evenings. It was my time as part of the rotation to work on Sabbath from 3:00 p.m. to 11:00 p.m. It became apparent to me that I needed to take the matter up with God. I needed to talk to Him.

I was forced to ask for outside help. I had to ask my pastor for help. He gave me a letter to take to my supervisor requesting my days off be changed. It was submitted to my supervisor. He said he would try to accommodate me if it was okay with my co-workers when he made the change. To my surprise, the schedule was made and the two other employees were pleased with the change. One of my friends said she

Lola Allen

629   If Any Little Word of Mine
8.7.8.7. With Refrain

Words by A. N. O. and F. E. B.   D. S. HAKES

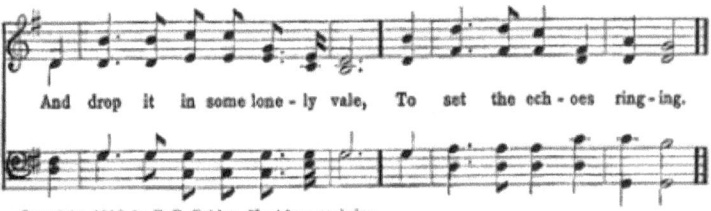

1. If an-y lit-tle word of mine May make a dark life bright-er,
2. If an-y lit-tle love of mine May make a hard life sweet-er,
3. If an-y lit-tle lift of mine May ease a toil-er bend-ing,

If an-y lit-tle song of mine May make a sad heart light-er,
If an-y lit-tle care of mine May make a friend's the fleet-er,
God give me love and care and strength; We live for Him by lend-ing.

Refrain

God help me speak the help-ing word, And sweet-en it with sing-ing,

And drop it in some lone-ly vale, To set the ech-oes ring-ing.

17   513

was happy to have Sundays to go to church with her daughter and take her to school on Monday mornings. And another young man was happy for his days because he played at a club at night after work.

It took a month for the schedule to change. I worked my last week on the Saturday schedule. I was supposed to work Thursday and be off Friday and Saturday. That never happened. That Thursday on my way to work is when my accident occurred. An accident that would forever change my life. I never returned to work from that day on. My death had been summoned, but God stepped in and saved my life by coming to the scene and my rescue in a thick cloud. I will never be the same. The date was October 1, 2009. Think about it! How would you see it? My circumstances forced me into retirement in an attempt to keep me from worship on Sabbath.

Congratulatory Remarks

To my mom,

I'm very proud of you. Even when the chips are down you still keep fighting to survive and keep the faith. You always believed in God, that He will take care of you. As for me being your son, I can say in my eyes and in my heart it's so true! Everything you have been preaching to me, over and over again, is true! All things are possible through Him. So, I say this to you mom. Congratulations on finishing your book !!! I love you with all my heart.

Love your son,
James Brown

To Ms. Lola Allen,

God is truly real and He is so faithful. He has inspired you to write your story as a testimony for others. Congratulations on your book and may your testimony encourage others to trust God and to look to Him for their needs and saving graces.

From,
Ms. Bertha Lewis, Miami FL

Congratulations to you Sis Allen on your upcoming book that you will be publishing. I want to wish you the best of luck, on the journey that you have been through since the incident. I understand the struggle, and I'm so excited for you and your book. This book will teach and show everyone that there is a God and He is real. He can do anything in His power to keep His people safe and secure. I want to say congrats again on your book Sis Allen, and I am giving you honor to mention my name in your book.

Roslyn Pinkney

You are brave. Your are strong. Your are loved. Sister Lola Allen, You are in my thoughts and in my heart.

Love,
Sheres Victor.

Lola Allen has gone through a lot and has looked to God for His help and guidance. I wish Lola all the best as she praises God for His goodness in her book.

Eileen John Lewis

Congratulations to Miss Lola Allen on reaching this very important milestone in her journey. This book that you have written has been a labour of love. It is truly a testament to your hard work and dedication. I thank God for your work and that you have been able to touch so many people with your caring and generous spirit over the years. Your strong belief in God and also your devotion to the ministry of the Seventh Day Adventist Church has been exemplary. Your vision is profound and has helped to inspire this book. Again, I thank God for your completed book and I hope it will be touch the lives of many people. May God bless you.

Thank you, with love
Nicole McIsaacs BSW

Sister Allen,

I wanted to congratulate you for persevering and following your vision to write and publish this book. May God continue to bless you and your family!

Your Brother In Christ,
Leonard O'Mara

Personal Prayer

Father, thank you for keeping me strong during difficult times in my life. Keep me strong in the confidence that absolutely nothing can defeat or change Your love for me. Father, help me to always follow Your divine plan for my life. Lord, when I feel I can do no more, give me the strength I need to hold on to my faith in You. Help me to always put You first in everything I do. When the future seems dark, help me to see and trust Your light through Jesus Christ my Lord.

Allen

NOTES

NOTES

NOTES

NOTES

NOTES

NOTES

NOTES

NOTES

NOTES

NOTES